LIGHTNING
BOLT
BOOKS™

Let's Visit the Desert

Buffy Silverman

Lerner Publications • Minneapolis

Lerner Publications Company
A division of Lerner Publishing Group, Inc.
241 First Avenue North
Minneapolis, MN 55401 USA

For reading levels and more information, look up this title at www.lernerbooks.com.

Library of Congress Cataloging-in-Publication Data

Names: Silverman, Buffy, author.
Title: Let's visit the desert / by Buffy Silverman.
Description: Minneapolis : Lerner Publications, [2017] | Series: Lightning bolt books. Biome explorers |
    Includes bibliographical references and index. | Audience: Age 5–8. | Audience: K to Grade 3.
Identifiers: LCCN 2015044360 (print) | LCCN 2016005018 (ebook) | ISBN 9781512411904 (lb : alk.
    paper) | ISBN 9781512412284 (pb : alk. paper) | ISBN 9781512411980 (eb pdf)
Subjects: LCSH: Deserts—Juvenile literature. | Desert ecology—Juvenile literature.
Classification: LCC GB612 .S55 2017 (print) | LCC GB612 (ebook) | DDC 577.54—dc23
LC record available at http://lccn.loc.gov/2015044360

Manufactured in the United States of America
1 – BP – 7/15/16

Table of Contents

A Journey to the Desert

Imagine a desert. Do you think of a hot, sandy habitat? Do you see a place with no plants or animals?

This desert has sand dunes. Dunes are mounds of sand. They are formed by the wind.

Some deserts are mostly sand. But others have stones on the ground. Plants can grow. Animals find food and make homes.

Many of the hottest places on Earth are deserts.

There are desert biomes
all around the world.
Deserts can be found on all
seven continents.

NORTH
AMERICA

EUROPE

ASIA

AFRICA

SOUTH
AMERICA

AUSTRALIA

Desert

ANTARCTICA

Deserts are dry. Rain and snow rarely fall. Some deserts are very hot. Rain evaporates quickly in the warm air.

Some deserts may get no rain for years.

Other deserts are cold.
Winters are long.

Snow and ice cover parts of polar deserts. Plants cannot use the frozen water.

Coastal deserts have cool winters and long, warm summers. Fog rolls in from the sea. But rain hardly ever falls.

The Atacama Desert in South America is a coastal desert.

Animals in the Desert

A roadrunner scoots across the rocky ground. The bird snaps up a lizard. Then it darts to a bush where its nest is hidden.

Roadrunners can dash more than 15 miles (24 kilometers) per hour.

Animals in a desert biome have special ways to get the water they need. Roadrunners get water from their food.

Roadrunners eat mostly small animals. Plants are a small part of their diet.

Tok-tokkie beetles live in coastal deserts. When fog appears, the beetles stand on their heads. Water from the fog collects on their backs. It drips into their mouths.

Many animals avoid the hot desert sun. In Australia, bilbies dig burrows with their strong claws. They stay underground all day.

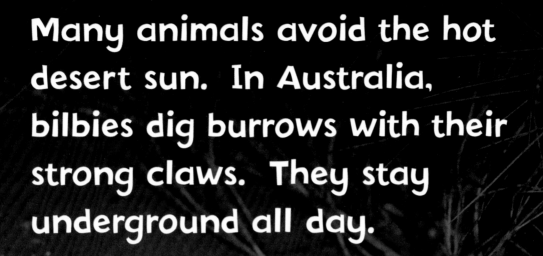

Bilby burrows can be up to 9.8 feet (3 meters) deep.

After sunset, the air is cooler. Bilbies come out at night. A bilby's big ears and sharp nose help it find food.

Kit foxes hunt for small animals such as rabbits and mice.

Kit foxes also spend most of the day underground. They lose heat through their long ears. They hunt during the cool night.

Spadefoot toads lay their eggs in desert ponds.

Many animals flock to desert ponds that fill when it rains. The ponds don't last long. They dry up under the hot sun.

Spadefoot toad eggs hatch in a couple of days. The baby toads are called tadpoles. The tadpoles grow quickly before ponds disappear.

Spadefoot toads bury themselves in the ground when ponds dry up. They wait for rain.

Plants in the Desert

Desert plants survive with little water. These ocotillo plants look like dead sticks. But they are alive.

To save water, these ocotillo plants will lose their leaves when the ground dries.

After a rainstorm, ocotillos grow green leaves. The leaves take in sunlight to make food for the plant. But the leaves

Seeds sprout when rain soaks a desert. Flowers carpet the ground. Plants quickly make seeds. A year or more may pass before another storm comes. Then the new seeds can sprout.

This cactus is called a prickly pear.

Some desert plants store water. A cactus's shallow roots suck water during a storm. The plant fills with water.

The cactus's waxy skin keeps water inside. Animals try to eat juicy cactuses. Prickly spines often stop the animals.

Other desert plants grow long roots. They reach far below to find water. Mesquite tree roots may reach more than 160 feet (49 m). That's as long as four large school buses!

Working Together

Plants and animals depend on one another in a desert ecosystem. Bats, birds, and insects carry pollen from flower to flower.

Pollen allows plants to make seeds.

Many animals eat desert plants.
Ants, mice, and lizards
search for seeds. Jackrabbits
graze on grass.

Other desert animals hunt. A snake hides in the shade of a rock. It lunges at a lizard.

Every plant, animal, and rock
plays its part in the desert.

People in the Desert

- People in the Atacama Desert use nets to get water. They set up giant nets to catch fog. Fog from the ocean collects on the nets. It forms water droplets. The water drips into pipes. The pipes carry water to tanks. People use it for drinking and for farming.

- Some cities are built on deserts. Tall buildings soar into the sky. These cities rely on water pumped from belowground. Some cities take salt out of ocean water. Then people can drink the water. People in deserts must use water carefully.

Biome Extremes

- **Driest desert:** The Atacama Desert. Some parts of this desert have not had rain for more than four hundred years.

- **Largest desert:** Antarctica

- **Oldest desert:** Namib Desert, Africa. The Namib Desert is at least fifty-five million years old.

- **Fastest runner:** Cheetahs in the Kalahari Desert are the fastest land animals on Earth. They can run about 60 miles (97 km) per hour!

- **Old-timer:** Welwitschia live for thousands of years. These plants grow only in the Namib Desert.

Glossary

biome: plants and animals in a large area, such as a desert or forest

coastal: along an ocean

desert: land that receives no more than 10 inches (25 centimeters) of rainfall in a year

ecosystem: an area of connected living and nonliving things

evaporate: to change from a liquid into a gas

fog: small drops of water floating in the air

habitat: the natural home of plants or animals

pollen: powder made by a flower. Pollen is carried to other flowers to make seeds.

Further Reading

ASDM Sonoran Desert Digital Library for Kids
http://www.desertmuseumdigitallibrary.org/kids

Fleisher, Paul. *Desert Food Webs in Action.* Minneapolis: Lerner Publications, 2014.

Fredericks, Anthony D. *Desert Night Desert Day.* Tucson: Rio Chico, 2011.

Plum Landing: Desert Videos
http://pbskids.org/plumlanding/video/desert.html

World Biomes: Desert
http://kids.nceas.ucsb.edu/biomes/desert.html

Zuehlke, Jeffrey. *The Grand Canyon.* Minneapolis: Lerner Publications, 2010.

Index

Photo Acknowledgments

The images in this book are used with the permission of: © Genevieve Vallee/Alamy, p. 2; © apdesign/Shutterstock.com, p. 4; © Anton Foltin/Shutterstock.com, pp. 5, 24; © Laura Westlund/Independent Picture Service, p. 6; © gkuna/Shutterstock.com, p. 7; © CoolKengzz/Shutterstock.com, p. 8; © Anderl/Shutterstock.com, p. 9; © All Canada Photos/Alamy, pp. 10, 16; © Robert Shantz/Alamy, p. 11; © Tierfotoagentur/Alamy, p. 12; © Martin Harvey/Getty Images, p. 13; © cbstockfoto/Alamy, p. 14; © Max Allen/Shutterstock.com, p. 15; © Danita Delimont/Alamy, p. 17; © iStockphoto.com/yenwen, p. 18; © Tom Roche/Shutterstock.com, p. 19; © Romiana Lee/Shutterstock.com, p. 20; © Konstantnin/Shutterstock.com, p. 21; © underworld/Shutterstock.com, p. 22; © Anke van Wyk/Shutterstock.com, p. 23; © Genevieve Vallee/Alamy, p. 24; © iStockphoto.com/EcoPic, p. 25; © John Cancalosi/Getty Images, p. 26; © Anton Foltin/Shutterstock.com, p. 27; © Sergey Uryadnikov/Shutterstock.com, p. 31.

Front cover: © iStockphoto.com/Ron Thomas.

Main body text set in Johann Light 30/36.